PENNSYLVANIA

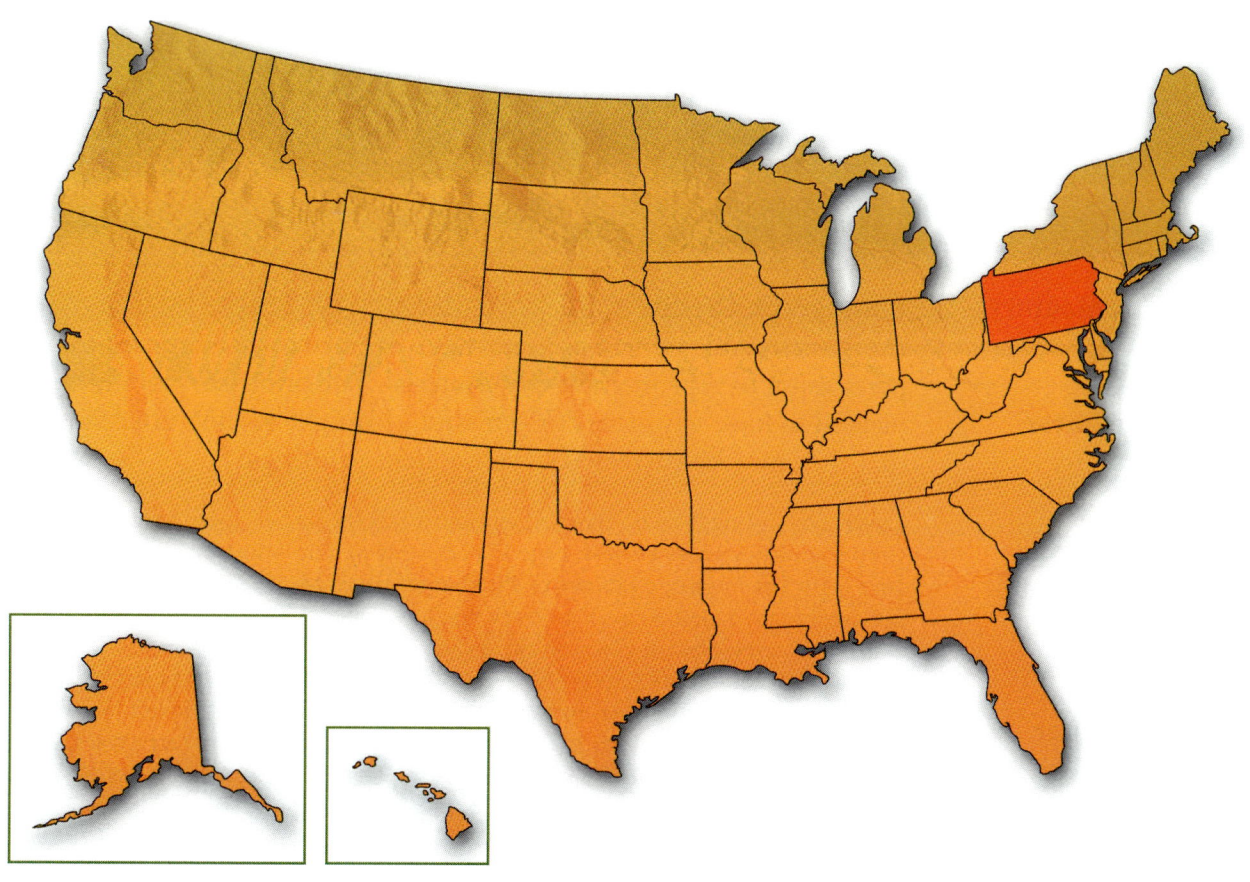

Natasha Evdokimoff

Published by Weigl Publishers Inc.
123 South Broad Street, Box 227
Mankato, MN 56002
USA
Web site: http://www.weigl.com
Copyright © 2001 WEIGL PUBLISHERS INC.
All rights reserved. No part of this publication may be reproduced, stored in a retrieval system, or transmitted in any form or by any means, electronic, mechanical, photocopying, recording, or otherwise, without the prior written permission of Weigl Publishers Inc.

Library of Congress Cataloging-in-Publication Data

Evdokimoff, Natasha.
    Pennsylvania / Natasha Evdokimoff.
      p. cm. -- (American states)
    Includes bibliographical references and index.
    ISBN 1-930954-06-9 (lib. bdg.)
    1. Pennsylvania--Juvenile literature. [1. Pennsylvania.] I. Title. II. Kid's guide to American states.

    F149.3 .E93 2001
    974.8--dc21
                                        00-049934

Printed in the United States of America
1 2 3 4 5 6 7 8 9 10 05 04 03 02 01

Project Coordinators
Rennay Craats
Michael Lowry
Substantive Editor
Carlotta Lemieux
Copy Editors
Heather Kissock
Jennifer Nault
Designers
Warren Clark
Terry Paulhus
Photo Researcher
Michael Lowry

Photograph Credits
Every reasonable effort has been made to trace ownership and to obtain permission to reprint copyright material. The publishers would be pleased to have any errors or omissions brought to their attention so that they may be corrected in subsequent printings.

Cover: Boy in Buggy (Jeff Hixon, Commonwealth Media Services), Leaves (Corel Corporation); **Archive Photos:** page 17; **Courtesy of The Atwater Kent Museum:** pages 16, 17, 19; **The Carnegie Library of Pittsburgh:** pages 18, 19; **Commonwealth Media Services:** pages 3 (Jeff Nixon), 4 (Terry Way), 5 (Mike Worley), 5 (Jeff Nixon), 6 (Jeff Nixon), 7 (Terry Way), 8 (Terry Way), 8 (Mike Worley), 9 (Terry Way), 11 (Chuck McDermott), 12 (Marty Ginter), 13 (Terry Way), 13 (Jeff Nixon), 14 (Jeff Nixon), 15 (Terry Way), 15 (Jeff Nixon), 16 (Mike Worley), 20 (Terry Way), 20 (Jeff Nixon), 21 (Terry Way), 22 (Jeff Nixon), 23 (Terry Way), 23 (Jeff Nixon), 24 (Terry Way), 25 (Terry Way), 27 (Mike Worley), 27 (Jeff Nixon); **Corel Corporation:** pages 10, 11, 14, 29; **Corbis Corporation:** pages 3, 9, 13, 14; **© Corbis/Magma:** pages 17 (Leonard de Selva), 18 (Francis G. Mayer), 25 (Hulton-Deutsch Collection); **EyeWire Corporation:** pages 8, 15, 24; **Alan Freed:** page 24; **Globe Photos Inc:** page 28 (Andrea Renault); **Government of Newfoundland and Labrador, Department of Forest Resources and Agrifoods:** page 11; **Kansas State Historical Society:** page 21; **Lawrence County Promotion Agency:** page 21; **Minnesota Historical Society:** page 16; **Pennsylvania Governor's Office:** pages 4, 6, 19; **Jim Steinhart of www.planetware.com:** page 29; **Reuters/Archive Photos:** pages 3 (Gary Caskey), 26 (Gary Caskey), 26 (Ray Stubblebine), 26 (Jason Cohn); **W. Lynn Seldon Jr.:** pages 4, 6, 7, 12, 20, 22, 23, 28; **Visuals Unlimited:** page 22 (Terry Ross).

CONTENTS

Introduction 4

Land and Climate 8

Natural Resources 9

Plants and Animals 10

Tourism 12

Industry 13

Goods and Services 14

First Nations 16

Explorers and Missionaries 17

Early Settlers 18

Population 20

Politics and Government 21

Cultural Groups 22

Arts and Entertainment 24

Sports 26

Brain Teasers 28

For More Information 30

Glossary 31

Index 32

4 American States

Independence Hall was restored in 1898 and is now a museum. Some of the original furniture is still inside.

INTRODUCTION

Pennsylvania means "Penn's Woodland." The name was given in honor of Admiral William Penn of England. The Admiral's son founded the colony in 1682. England had already laid claim to the land, and the King of England gave the land to Admiral Penn as payment for a loan.

The state has a rich political history. During the American Revolution, Pennsylvania was the center of action. The Declaration of Independence was signed there on July 4, 1776. Later, a famous Civil War battle was fought in Pennsylvania. The Battle of Gettysburg was an important victory for the North. As a result of heavy losses at Gettysburg, the South would never again be able to launch a major attack against the North.

Quick Facts

The state motto is "Virtue, Liberty, and Independence."

Pennsylvania became the second official state on December 12, 1787.

Philadelphia is the state's largest city.

The state seal is a shield with a sailing ship, plow, and wheat bundles on it.

The state flag bears the official coat of arms on a background of Old Glory blue.

The historic Gettysburg battlefield serves as a reminder of the heavy losses suffered in the Civil War.

Introduction

The United States *Brig Niagara* is the official flagship of Pennsylvania. Its home port is Erie.

Getting There

Pennsylvania is in the Middle Atlantic region. New York borders the north and shares the east border with New Jersey. The southern border states are Delaware, Maryland, and West Virginia. West Virginia shares the western border with Ohio. The Delaware River and Lake Erie are water boundaries around the state.

Pennsylvania is served by 119,281 miles of public highway and 5,196 miles of railroad track. The state is also serviced by 463 airports.

Pennsylvania is nicknamed the Keystone State. To be a keystone means to be at the center of something. The nickname represents the state's central role in the formation of the United States. It also stands for Pennsylvania's location among the original thirteen states.

Quick Facts

Smaller cities in the state are Allentown, Bethlehem, Erie, Reading, Scranton, and Lancaster.

The Mason–Dixon Line, which separated the North from the South, was established with Maryland in 1769.

The first covered bridge in the country was built over the Schuylkill River in Philadelphia in 1805.

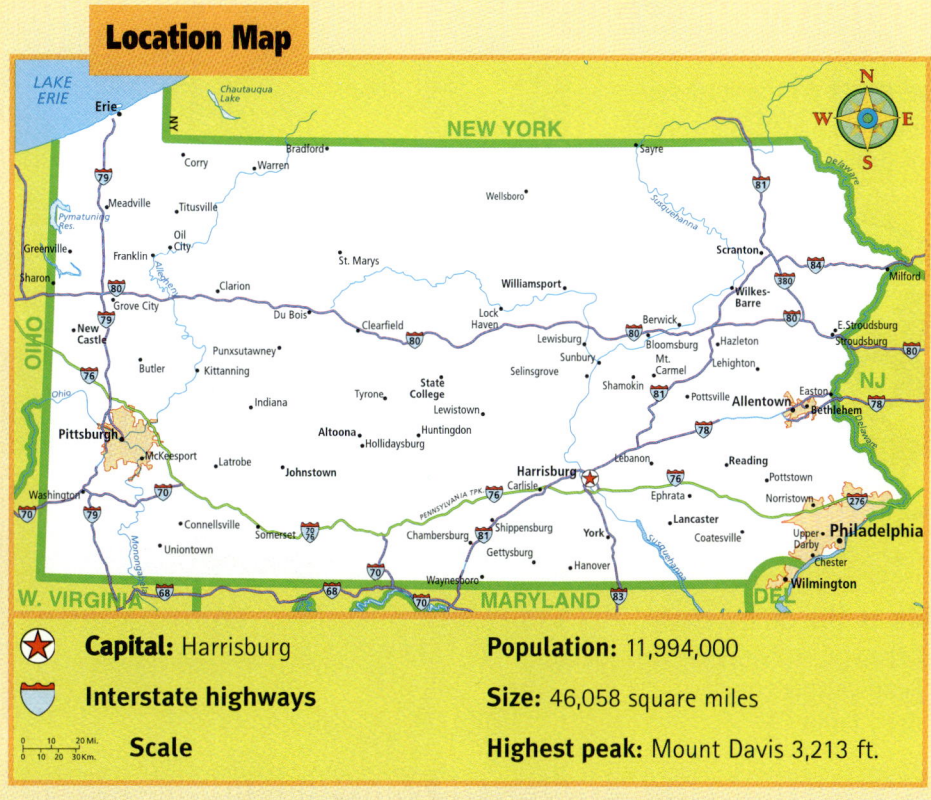

Location Map

Capital: Harrisburg
Interstate highways
Scale
Population: 11,994,000
Size: 46,058 square miles
Highest peak: Mount Davis 3,213 ft.

6   American States

Pennsylvania was one of the original thirteen states in the Union. It was the center of government from 1776 to 1800. Laws passed in that time formed the basis of the United States government today.

Modern day Pennsylvania is a busy and diverse place. Citizens of the state work in a variety of areas, from farming to **high-technology** manufacturing. In addition to the many historical sites, the state's beautiful countryside and mountains make Pennsylvania a treat to visit.

Historical guides take visitors on tours of Pennsylvania's past. Tour guides wear costumes to give visitors a sense of early colonial life.

In the fall, Lake Naomi explodes with stunning autumn colors.

Quick Facts

The crest of the state seal is an eagle, which is a symbol of strength and purity.

Milk is the official state beverage, in honor of Pennsylvania's many dairy farms.

INTRODUCTION 7

Beautifully cared for farms can be found in the Pennsylvania Dutch farming region.

Harrisburg has been the state capital since 1812. Past capital cities include Philadelphia and Lancaster. Over time, Pittsburgh and Philadelphia have become the two most populated **urban** centers in the state. Philadelphia's population is the fifth highest in the country, behind New York City, Los Angeles, Chicago, and Houston. Despite its cities, Pennsylvania has not lost its **rural** charm. The state is still largely covered by farmland and forests. Pennsylvania has the highest rural population of the nation.

The city of Pittsburgh is known for being comfortable, affordable, and safe.

QUICK FACTS

The state measures 46,058 square miles.

Although well populated, Pennsylvania is quite small. The state ranks thirty-third in size among all states.

Betsy Ross was a native Pennsylvanian. She is reported to have sewn the first United States flag in 1776. The original flag consisted of thirteen stripes and thirteen stars.

LAND AND CLIMATE

Pennsylvania has a varied landscape. The highest point is Mount Davis at 3,213 feet. The lowest point is at sea level along the Delaware River. The land in Pennsylvania changes from sandy plains to farmland and from valleys to mountains.

There are three major rivers in the state—the Delaware, the Susquehanna, and the Ohio. Dams are used to generate **hydroelectric power** and provide drinking water. Pennsylvania also has many lakes which formed when the glaciers melted nearly 10,000 years ago.

The climate in Pennsylvania is humid with plenty of rainfall. There are distinct weather changes for each season. The different regions have different temperatures. Pennsylvania's north is cooler than the south. The southeastern part of the state enjoys long summers and mild winters, while the uplands to the north have short summers and harsh winters. The average state temperature in the summer is 70 °Fahrenheit. In the winter months, the average temperature is 30 °F.

QUICK FACTS

The growing season varies between three and seven months, depending on the region.

Pine Creek Gorge is known as "Pennsylvania's Grand Canyon."

Pennsylvania is divided into seven regions: the Atlantic Coastal Plain, the Peidmont, the South Mountain, the Reading Prong, the Ridge and Valley, the Allegheny Plateaus, and the Lake Erie Lowland.

Pine Creek Gorge is 50 miles long and 1,200 feet deep. Pine Creek is the largest creek in the United States.

GEOGRAPHY

NATURAL RESOURCES

Natural resources have always been important to Pennsylvania's economy. Coal, oil, and natural gas are the state's leading resources.

Coal mines have operated in the state for more than 200 years. Most **manufacturers** used to burn coal for heat and energy. The state led the nation in coal production for many decades. Since then, concerns about pollution have caused the coal industry to decline. Pennsylvania is now ranked fourth in coal output among all states.

Oil has been produced in the state since 1859. Pennsylvania produced 2 million barrels of oil in 1998. Natural gas is a **by-product** of oil. Natural gas is an efficient way to produce electricity. In 1998, Pennsylvania produced 1.9 billion cubic meters of natural gas.

Oil rigs are used to drill for oil that is found beneath the surface of the earth.

QUICK FACTS

Coal was the main fuel used to **smelt** iron in the 1880s.

The world's first commerical oil well was drilled in Pennsylvania in 1859.

Limestone is a common mineral in Pennsylvania. It is often used in the making of cement.

Coal mining drills are normally about 200 feet long and between 2 and 7 feet wide.

PLANTS AND ANIMALS

Pennsylvania is very green due to its large number of trees. The state has close to 20 million acres of forest. White pine, beech, and sugar maple trees are found in the north. White oak, chestnut, and hickory trees are found in the south. Pennsylvania's state tree is the hemlock.

Cranberries flourish in Pennsylvania's marshy areas, and blueberry bushes grow well on the state's rocky hillsides. Flowers are also plentiful. Colorful violets, mountain laurels, and lady-slippers grow across the state.

The large forests provide shelter for many animals. Raccoons, squirrels, rabbits, skunks, and woodchucks are common. Deer, black bears, and coyotes also make their home in the forests. Fortunately, state **gaming** laws protect many wild animals from **poachers**.

Quick Facts

The mountain laurel, which is in full bloom in mid-June, is the state flower.

The white-tailed deer is the official state animal.

Black bears were once nearly extinct in Pennsylvania. Now, thanks to game laws, there are many roaming the state.

The coyote is a swift hunter that can reach speeds of up to 40 miles per hour.

GEOGRAPHY

In 1997, the Pennsylvania Wildlife Center opened in Verona. The Center takes in injured wildlife. Once the animal has healed, it is released back into the wild.

Lakes and rivers are well stocked with fish. Trout, perch, pike, bass, and catfish swim in the state's waters. **Amphibians** and reptiles, including salamanders and snakes, are found in the damp northern areas.

Pennsylvania is home to many kinds of birds. Birdwatchers admire robins, cardinals, and mockingbirds. The state bird is the ruffed grouse. Sometimes called partridges, grouse are large wild birds. Their reddish-brown color makes it easy for them to hide in bushes.

The Pennsylvania Wildlife Center has treated over 400 animals since 1997.

Quick Facts

The Ohio River makes up 35 percent of the water that drains into the Gulf of Mexico.

Pennsylvania has 116 state parks.

The male ruffed grouse is known for the loud drumming noise it makes by beating its wings rapidly in the air.

12 AMERICAN STATES

TOURISM

Gettysburg National Military Park holds battle re-enactments of the Civil War.

QUICK FACTS

The Pennsylvania Turnpike was the nation's first highway. It crosses the state from east to west.

More than 1.5 million people visit the Liberty Bell in Philadelphia every year.

Pennsylvania has some of the most historic sites in the country. Millions of tourists visit them every year. Tourism brings $6 billion into the state of Pennsylvania each year.

The Liberty Bell is one of the biggest tourist attractions. The Liberty Bell has rung on many historic occasions, including to signal the first reading of the Declaration of Independence.

Independence Hall is another popular attraction. The Declaration of Independence and the American Constitution were drafted there. Famous Americans, such as George Washington and Andrew Hamilton, worked in Independence Hall.

National military parks also attract tourists. The Gettysburg and Valley Forge parks are the most famous. The Battle of Gettysburg played a key role in the Civil War. Troops from the thirteen colonies camped at Valley Forge during the American Revolution.

People also visit the Pennsylvania Dutch farming region to see the **Amish** way of life. The Amish are a religious group. They live a simple, farm-based life without the assistance of modern technology.

The push-scooter is a popular form of transportation among Amish children.

ECONOMY 13

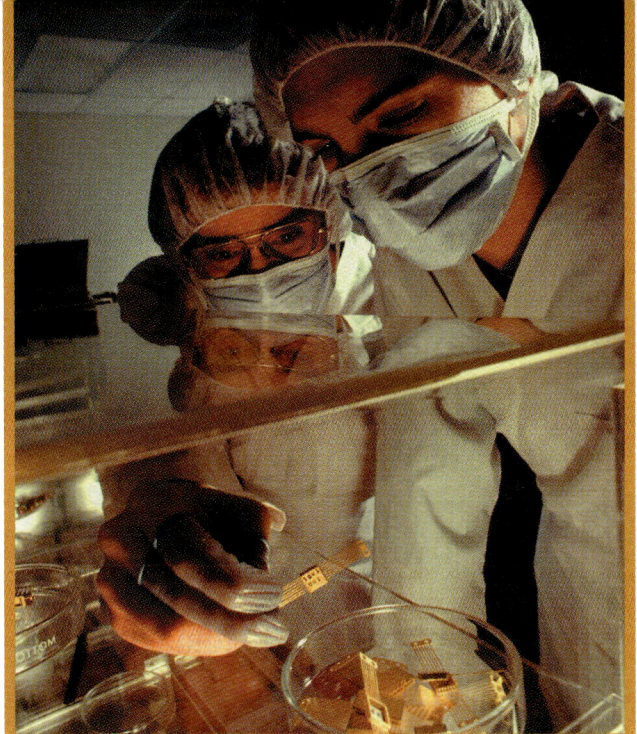

Rooms used to make computer parts must be free of dust, which can ruin the electronics.

INDUSTRY

Lumber was Pennsylvania's first modern industry. Loggers cut down trees for wood. When forests began to decline, lumber production was nearly stopped. Recent **reforestation** has revived the lumber industry.

Steel production was Pennsylvania's main industry for many years. The state supplied half of the nation's steel for the Civil War. Today, the steel industry is much smaller. Even so, the state is still a leader of steel production in the country.

Electronics have now taken over as Pennsylvania's major industry. The state is a top manufacturer of computer **components** and high-technology systems. Medicine is another modern industry. Prescription drugs are made in the state for use around the world.

QUICK FACTS

The Conestoga wagon was developed in Lancaster County. It was the model used for the wagons in America's western **migration**. The wagon could carry 4 tons.

Pennsylvania is home to one of the United States' mint operations.

The state's nine nuclear power plants produce one-third of its electricity.

In 1840, Pennsylvania was the home of more newspapers than any other state.

Old sawmills are a reminder of Pennsylvania's early logging industry. Mills were built on rivers downstream of the logging area.

14 American States

GOODS AND SERVICES

The soil in Pennsylvania is fertile and ideal for many crops. The state has about 9 million acres of working farmland. Dairy products are some of the state's most important exports. Dairy farms are most common in the northern part of the state. Here, milk is turned into cheese, yogurt, and ice cream. Some Pennsylvania farms raise livestock, while others grow grains and vegetables.

Pennsylvania also grows a variety of fruits. Apples and peaches are grown on southeast mountain slopes. Cherries, apples, and grapes grow near Lake Erie. As this area gets little frost, it is an ideal place to grow fruit.

Other state products are poultry, eggs, corn, potatoes, mushrooms, beans, and wheat. Winter wheat, which is used to make fine pastry and cake flour, is an important crop in Pennsylvania's southeast. Buckwheat, which does not need a long growing season, is an important northeastern crop.

Quick Facts

Pennsylvania's railroad system was essential for transporting goods during the Civil War.

Pennsylvania was home to the country's first hospital, library, and insurance company.

Cheddar cheese is the most popular type of cheese in the world.

Economy 15

Quick Facts

The state is ranked fifth in the country for its total number of milking cows.

In 1999, there were 59,000 farms in Pennsylvania.

Other important crops in the state include potatoes, oats, rye, and barley.

Pretzels, potato chips, and sausages are among the state's exports.

The state is also known for its maple syrup and Christmas trees. The sale of all farm products brings $3.3 billion into the state every year.

Many Pennsylvanians work in manufacturing. Food processing has become an important industry in Pennsylvania. Chocolate and cocoa are the leading products, as well as ice cream and canned mushrooms.

Jobs in the service industry are also growing rapidly. More than 33 percent of Pennsylvania's population works in the service industry. Some of the key service areas are entertainment, health care, and retail.

Pennsylvania is well known for its high level of medical research.

Giant towers, called silos, are used to store grains and food for farm animals.

16 American States

FIRST NATIONS

There were three main groups of First Nations peoples in early Pennsylvania—the Delawares, Susquehannocks, and Shawnees.

The Delaware people lived by the Delaware River. They called themselves Leni Lenape, meaning original people. They fought for the British in the American Revolution. Under the pressure of new settlers, the Delaware began to move west and north. The Delaware's **descendants** now live in Oklahoma and Canada.

The Susquehannock were a powerful tribe that lived along the Susquehanna River. Illnesses brought by settlers had a devastating impact on the group. Over the years, wars with the Iroquois virtually eliminated the tribe. In 1763, the remaining twenty Susquehannocks were murdered by settlers who were angered by **Pontiac's War**.

The Shawnee people came from the west around 1690. They settled on the banks of Pennsylvania's rivers. During periods of war, the group **allied** themselves with either French or British troops. Over time, they moved to Oklahoma.

Quick Facts

Native Americans and settlers lived in peace for many years. Later, conflicts over the settlement of Native American lands resulted in the forced migration of many Native American peoples.

Early First Nations groups made tools and weapons from wood and bark.

Native Americans taught early settlers to fish, hunt, and farm. They also showed settlers trade routes through the region.

Important Shawnee ceremonies include the green corn dance, the autumn bread dance, and the spring bread dance.

EXPLORERS AND MISSIONARIES

James II later became king of Great Britain. He was overthrown from the throne in the Glorious Revolution of 1688.

Swedish explorers made the first settlement in Pennsylvania in the 1600s. They settled by the Delaware River on Tinicum Island near present-day Philadelphia and called the area New Sweden. Not long after, Dutch explorers took over the region and changed the name to New Netherland. By 1655, the Dutch controlled most of the area.

About ten years later, under the reign of James II, the duke of York, British forces claimed the Pennsylvania area for England. They renamed the entire region New York. From this land, the colonies of New York, New Jersey, Pennsylvania, and Delaware were later created.

QUICK FACTS

- **Johan Printz** was the governor of New Sweden in 1643. This area later became Pennsylvania.
- **Captain John Smith** sailed up the Susquehanna River in 1608 to explore the territory.
- **Philadelphia became** the center of British life in the New World.

New Sweden was the only Swedish colony to be established in America.

18 AMERICAN STATES

EARLY SETTLERS

Quakers were often arrested because of their religion.

The founder of modern-day Pennsylvania was William Penn. Penn was a religious man and a member of the Society of Friends, or **Quakers**. As a religious group, Quakers were not accepted in England. They were **persecuted** for their beliefs. Penn saw the new land as a place for all people to live in peace and practice their religions.

While still in England, Penn wrote the Pennsylvania Frame of Government. This document outlined the laws for the new colony. Penn sent his cousin, William Markham, to the colony to make sure the laws were upheld in the new land. By the time William Penn arrived from England, the colony was already taking shape. His Frame of Government promised religious freedom and fair laws. People came from many countries, including Germany and Holland, to live in the new free land.

QUICK FACTS

- **William Penn was** born on October 24, 1644, in England.
- **Penn called his** new territory a "holy experiment" in religious freedom.
- **King Charles II** signed the Charter of Pennsylvania in 1681.

William Penn built up goodwill with Native Americans through a series of treaties.

The Past

As more religious migrants came to Pennsylvania, churches sprang up across the land.

English and Welsh Quakers came to join Penn's group. They settled around Philadelphia. German settlers began cultivating the farmland now called Pennsylvania Dutch country. A large portion of these Germans were Amish and Mennonite groups who were attracted to the area by Penn's promise of religious freedom.

Around 1718, large numbers of Scottish and Irish people arrived. **Famine** and religious hardships in their homelands prompted them to seek new places to live. These groups colonized the Cumberland Valley.

The Pennsylvania colony grew quickly, as settlers from Connecticut, Maryland, and Virginia moved to the area. There were about 20,000 residents in 1700. This number grew to 300,000 by 1776. Many of the religious and cultural traditions of the early settlers are still practiced in the state today.

Quick Facts

The *Brig Niagara* and five other ships were built in the small town of Erie. The *Brig Niagara* played an important role in the War of 1812.

In 1984, William Penn and his wife Hannah were made honorary United States citizens.

The four-wheeled buggy wagon is still used by the Amish. According to Amish tradition, modern forms of transportation are forbidden.

POPULATION

Every July, Lawrence County celebrates at the Fireworks Festival.

Pennsylvania is well populated considering its small size. In 1999, the population was nearly 12 million. The state has the fifth highest population in the country. Only California, New York, Texas, and Florida have larger populations.

About 69 percent of the state's citizens live in cities, the most populated of which is Philadelphia. The other 31 percent of citizens live in rural areas. Pennsylvania has the highest rural population in the country.

Pennsylvania has a high proportion of senior citizens. Only Florida and West Virginia have older populations. Pennsylvanian women outnumber the men in the state by almost 500,000.

Quick Facts

Pennsylvania's population has changed little since the 1940s.

There are 268 people per square mile in the state.

Philadelphia's harbor is one of the largest fresh water ports in the world.

CULTURE 21

POLITICS AND GOVERNMENT

Along with Virginia, Kentucky, and Massachusetts, Pennsylvania is a commonwealth state. This term means "for the common good" or "shared well being." This English title was given back in the days of Pennsylvania's first constitution. Today, it is an honorary title. The words state and commonwealth can be interchanged.

Pennsylvania has had four constitutions. The present constitution came into effect in 1874. Any **amendments** to the constitution are proposed by the **legislature**.

Several female political **activists** came from Pennsylvania. Lucretia Mott, Ann Davies, and others argued for women's rights. Together they helped bring women the right to vote. Independence Hall was also the location of Susan B. Anthony's famous reading of the "Declaration of Rights for Women."

As a result of its high population, Pennsylvania is well represented in the federal House of Representatives, with twenty-one members. Two United States senators are also elected from Pennsylvania.

The Harrisburg State Capitol was modeled after St. Peter's Church in Rome.

Quick Facts

There are sixty-seven counties in the state.

Pennsylvania has 50 members in the state Senate and 203 members in the House of Representatives.

Women obtained the right to vote in Pennsylvania in August 1920.

22 American States

CULTURAL GROUPS

Amish-produced goods are valued for their high quality.

Quick Facts

Amish women do not wear jewelry.

The oldest Amish order lives in Lancaster County. About 18,000 members make up the Lancaster group.

Amish children attend school only through to the eighth grade.

Amish brides wear blue at their weddings.

The Amish way of life is the same today as it was centuries ago.

A well-established group in Pennsylvania today is the Amish. Their beliefs are grounded in **modesty**, family, and community. Their homes do not have electricity. Amish people grow their own food and make their own materials and clothing.

Clothing sets the Amish apart. Women and girls wear plain cotton dresses and aprons. Men and boys wear dark suits and cotton shirts. Women wear prayer caps and men wear straw hats. Modest dress is an expression of their faith. They believe that clothing should not draw attention or be boastful.

Most Amish people speak three languages. Their native language is German. After years in the United States, their language changed. They speak a German **dialect** called Pennsylvania Dutch at home. In church, the Amish speak High German, a more formal form of the language. English is learned in school and is spoken whenever dealing with people outside the group.

Amish people work together to construct buildings in their communities.

Culture 23

Swedish clothing is brightly colored with embroidered patterns.

The Scandinavian culture is also represented in the state. Scandinavian people came from northern Europe in the 1600s. The first Scandinavian settlers in the state were the Swedish. Other Scandinavian countries are Denmark, Finland, Iceland, and Norway. Each Scandinavian country has its own language. While Finnish is a very different language, the Danish, Swedish, and Norwegian languages are similar and are usually understood among each group.

Today, the Scandinavian Society of Pennsylvania promotes traditional activities in the Pittsburgh area. Celebrations include folk festivals with cultural song and dance. Traditional clothing is worn such as heavy wool jackets and vests, and sometimes wooden clogs. Sausages, meatballs, cheese, and flatbread are foods usually served at these gatherings.

Quick Facts

More than 100 different religious groups live in the state.

During the 20th Century, many African Americans migrated to Pennsylvania.

Souvenirs, hotdogs, hamburgers, and soft drinks are forbidden at the Goschenhoppen Folk Festival.

The German Goschenhoppen Folk Festival features traditional German crafts, clothing, and foods.

24 American States

ARTS AND ENTERTAINMENT

In the past, attendance at Groundhog Day has been as high as 30,000.

Quick Facts

The first radio station in the world was KDKA in Pittsburgh.

Philadelphia has been called the "Athens of America" because of its rich cultural life.

The first motion-picture theater in the world opened in Pittsburgh in 1905.

The eyes of the country look to Pennsylvania every February 2. On Groundhog Day, the town of Punxsutawney comes alive. Everyone waits to hear whether Punxsutawney Phil, the groundhog, will see his shadow. Legend has it that if Phil sees his shadow, there will be six more weeks of winter. If he does not, people can expect an early spring. Thousands of people from neighboring areas travel to Punxsutawney to join the festivities.

Pennsylvania's performing arts community has its own avenue to call home. The Avenue of the Arts in Philadelphia is a world class cultural hot spot. The Avenue is home to ballets, operas, theaters, and music halls.

Pennsylvanian musicians have a chance to show off their talents at the open house festival on the Avenue of the Arts.

CULTURE 25

The Barnes Foundation was started by Dr. Albert C. Barnes in order to promote the fine arts.

The Philadelphia Festival of World Cinema runs every May. For two weeks, theaters showcase international and independent movies. If the movie is in another language, subtitles translate the words at the bottom of the screen.

The National Liberty Museum is in Philadelphia. Inside, **patrons** can find beautiful glass sculptures, paintings, and interactive artwork. The museum was founded to celebrate national **diversity**. Art exhibits express freedom and tolerance for others.

Pennsylvania is also renowned in the world of dance. The Pennsylvania Ballet was founded in 1964 and is known for its wonderful productions.

Because of its excellent acoustics, the Music Hall of the Andrew Carnegie Free Library is often used for musical concert recordings.

QUICK FACTS

The Orpheus Club of Philadelphia is one of the first national music organizations.

The Warner brothers of movie fame started their careers in Pennsylvania.

26 American States

SPORTS

The Philadelphia Flyers were once nicknamed the Broad Street Bullies because of their toughness.

Sports fans in Pennsylvania have much to enjoy. Professional baseball, hockey, basketball, and football are all played in the state. Philadelphia and Pittsburgh both have professional teams. Philadelphia teams include the Flyers on the ice, the 76ers on the basketball court, the Eagles on the football field, and the Phillies on the baseball diamond.

In Pittsburgh, the National Hockey League boasts the Penguins, and the National Football League hosts the Steelers. The Pittsburgh Pirates represent Pennsylvania in Major League Baseball. Having more than one team per league makes for exciting cross-state rivalry.

The Pittsburgh Steelers have won the Super Bowl four times.

Quick Facts

The University of Pennsylvania held its first classes in 1740.

The Philadelphia Phillies are the oldest professional sports team to have kept the same name and the same city throughout their entire history.

CULTURE 27

The Delaware Water Gap is a great spot for canoeing.

Universities and colleges across the state have sports teams for men and women. Almost every sport imaginable is played at college level. Action-packed games draw thousands of fans to cheer on the home team.

Outdoor sports are great for those who like to participate rather than watch. There are many places in Pennsylvania to enjoy the outdoors. Among the most popular sporting activities are fishing, swimming, hiking, and golf. The Pocono Mountains and Delaware Water Gap are two popular spots. Winter brings snow to the mountain regions where many people ski. Snowshoeing and sledding are also popular winter activities.

Fly-fishing is a specialized form of fishing.

In 1939, Little League Baseball was founded in Williamsport, Pennsylvania, with only three teams. There are now over 7,000 Little League teams around the world.

QUICK FACTS

Baseball great Reggie Jackson was born in Wyncote, Pennsylvania.

Every August, Willamsport hosts the Little League Baseball World Series.

American States

Brain Teasers

1 Independence Hall was more than the first place of government. What other purpose did it once serve?

Answer: The basement of Independence Hall was once the city dog pound.

2 When did the Liberty Bell crack?

Answer: Some historians say that the bell cracked the first time it was rung! This has not been proven. It is agreed that the last time the bell rang was on George Washington's birthday in 1846. After that, the crack was too big to ever ring the bell again.

3 What Pennsylvania rodent has famous friends?

Answer: Punxsutawney Phil, the groundhog, has met many famous people. Phil traveled to Washington to meet President Reagan. He starred in a movie with actor Bill Murray and even appeared on Oprah Winfrey in 1995.

4 Pennsylvania was given to William Penn as payment from King James II. How much did the king owe?

Answer: The king owed Admiral Penn £16,000. In today's dollars that would be more than $240,000 US.

ACTIVITIES 29

5 What is the biggest natural lake in the state?

Answer: Conneaut Lake, in Crawford County.

6 What cost $110,168.05 to build in 1791?

Answer: The First Bank of the United States. The bank was built in Philadelphia to create one national currency.

7 What Pennsylvania city is nicknamed the "Christmas City?"

Answer: Bethlehem

8 Pennsylvania is known as the Keystone State. What other nickname does the state have?

Answer: Pennsylvania is also called the Quaker State because its founder was a member of the Quakers.

FOR MORE INFORMATION

Books

Kent, Deborah. *America the Beautiful: Pennsylvania*. Chicago: Children's Press, 1988.

Swain, Gwenyth. *Pennsylvania*. Minneapolis: Lerner Publications, 1994.

Fradin, Dennis Brindell. *Pennsylvania*. Chicago: Children's Press, 1994.

Aylesworth, Jim. *Folks in the Valley, A Pennsylvania Dutch ABC*. New York: HarperCollins, 1992.

Web Sites

You can also go online and have a look at the following Web sites:
Stately Knowledge
http://www.ipl.org/youth/stateknow/pa1.html

Pennsylvania State Homepage
http://www.state.pa.us

Pennsylvania State Agencies for Kids
http://www.state.pa.us/kids/

Virtual Tour of Historic Philadelphia
http://www.ushistory.org/tour/_oldcity.html

Punxsutawney Phil Homepage
http://www.punxsutawneyphil.com

Some Web sites stay current longer than others. To find other Pennsylvania Web sites, enter search terms such as "Pennsylvania," "Pittsburgh," "Gettysburg," or any other topic you want to research.

GLOSSARY

activists: people who fight for a cause

allied: to side with another group or country

amendments: changes made to an important document

Amish: a conservative Christian group

amphibians: cold-blooded animals capable of living on land and in water

brig: a sailing ship with two masts

by-product: a substance that comes from another related product

components: parts of an electronic system

descendants: relatives

dialect: any special variety of a language

diversity: variety; differences

famine: widespread hunger

gaming: hunting wild animals, birds, or fish

high-technology: having very modern qualities, usually electronic based

hydroelectric power: energy created by moving water

legislature: a group of people with the power to make or change laws

manufacturers: producers of goods

migration: movement from one land area to another

modesty: not showing off oneself or one's talents

patrons: people who support a group or activity

persecuted: being attacked for one's beliefs

poachers: people who hunt animals illegally

Pontiac's War: Chief Pontiac organized many Native American tribes in an attempt to drive back British forces

Quakers: a religious group with European origins

reforestation: replanting trees to replace those cut down

rural: relating to the country; farming based

smelt: to melt or fuse together at a very hot temperature

urban: relating to the city

INDEX

American Revolution 4, 12, 16
Amish 12, 19, 22, 31
Anthony, Susan B. 21

Bethlehem 5, 29

Civil War 4, 12, 13, 14
coal 9
commonwealth 21

Declaration of Independence 4, 12
Delawares 16

farming 6, 7, 12, 14, 15
flowers 10

Gettysburg 4, 12, 30

Harrisburg 5, 7, 21

Independence Hall 4, 12, 21, 28
iron 9

keystone 5, 29
King James II 17, 28

Liberty Bell 12, 28

military parks 12

Native Americans (First Nations) 16, 18
natural gas 9

Ohio River 8, 11
oil 9

Penn, William 4, 18, 19, 28
Pennsylvania Dutch 12, 19, 22, 30
Philadelphia 4, 5, 7, 12, 17, 19, 20, 24, 25, 26, 29, 30
Pittsburgh 7, 23, 24, 26, 30
Punxsutawney Phil 24, 28, 30

Quakers 18, 19, 29, 31

rivers 11, 13, 16, 17

Shawnees 16
steel 13
Susquehannocks 16

temperature 8
trees 10, 13, 15

Valley Forge 12

Washington, George 12, 28
wildlife 10, 11